MY CLASS
VISITS A
MUSEUM

MY CLASS VISITS A
MUSEUM

Vivien Griffiths

meets

Lorraine Copes

Photography: Maggie Murray

Franklin Watts

London/New York/Toronto/Sydney

14552

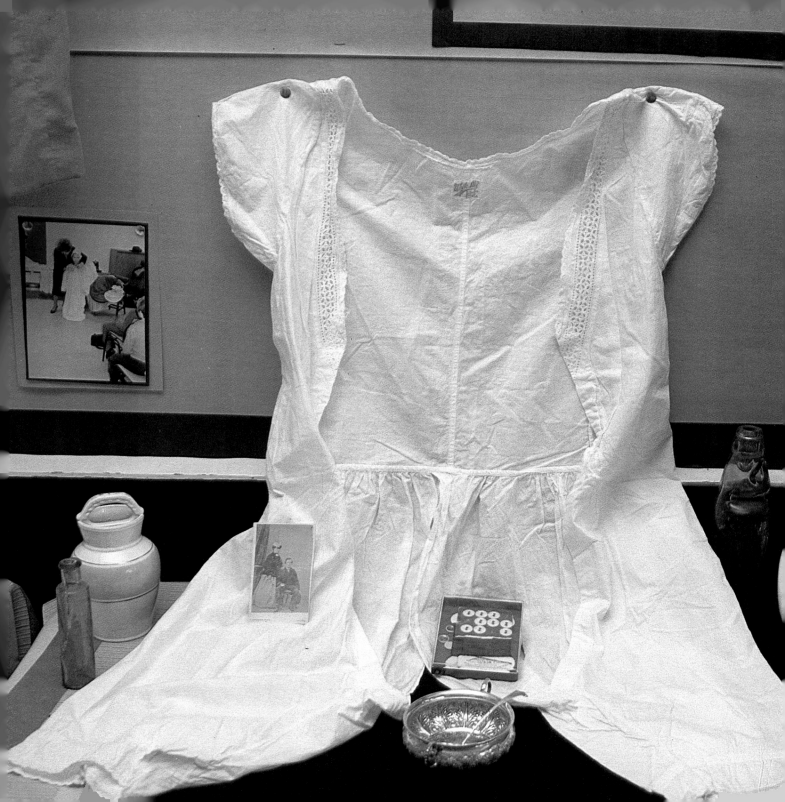

This term our project is all about time.
We try to imagine
what it was like to live
a hundred years ago.

Some of our mums and dads
bring old things to school
for everyone to see.
Mohammed is winding up an old clock.

We all write our names with a quill pen.
It's made from a feather,
which we dip in the ink.

Today we are going to visit the museum in town
so we can see what people used to wear.
Mrs Peate meets us.
She takes us around the museum.

First of all,
we have to look
at some paintings.

These people are going
to the seaside on a train.
They must be very hot
in those heavy clothes.

This painting shows lots of different people in London.
Can you tell which people are rich and which are poor?

Then Mrs Peate shows us some clothes,
which she tells us are a hundred years old.
She puts a nightdress and cap on Aprill.

Sheryl is wearing a pinafore dress,
made of rough cotton.
It probably belonged to a servant girl.

Jessica is wearing a silk crinoline
with a bustle, which sticks out at the back.

Some rich men wore suits
and bowler hats
to go to work.

When they were at home,
they sometimes wore
velvet hats.

A high collar, like this,
must have been very hard
to button up.

So were these gaiters,
which stopped mud
from splashing
on to men's trousers.
They had to be put on
with a button hook.

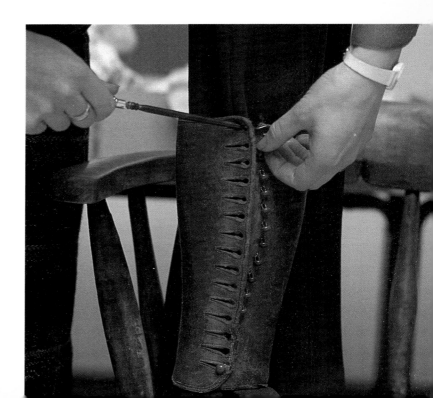

Rich people could buy
soft leather shoes.

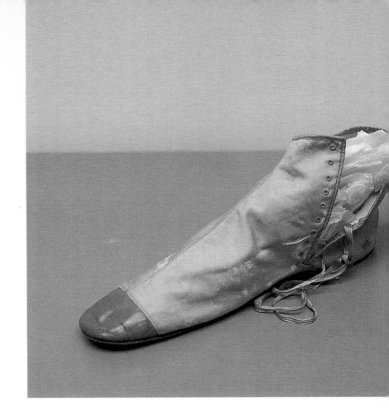

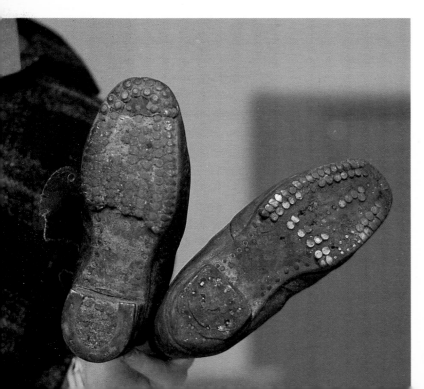

Poor people could
only afford heavy boots.

Can you see the big nails,
which they put in the soles,
to make them last longer?

Vincent tries on a sailor suit.
He has to jump up and down to get it on.

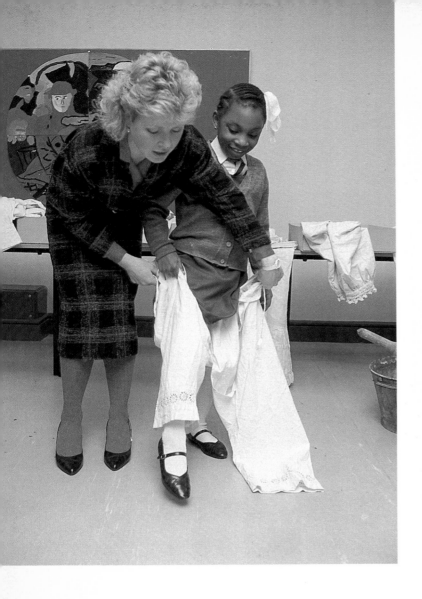

Mrs Peate dresses me up as a Victorian lady. These huge knickers are called drawers.

Next comes the camisole and then the stays.

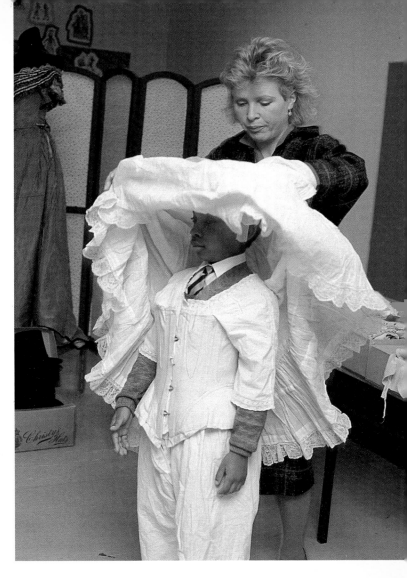

The strings on the stays are pulled very tight because it was the fashion then to have tiny waists.

A real Victorian lady would have worn nine or ten petticoats. I am only wearing one.

The crinoline is next,

and last of all, the top
and overskirt.
I'm getting very hot now.

When I try to sit down,
you can see what happens!

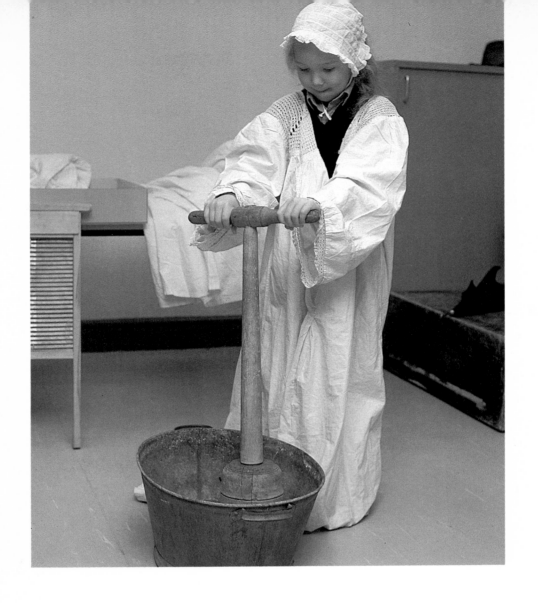

On washday, clothes were swished
up and down with a wooden "wash-dolly".
People didn't wash clothes very often,
so sometimes they were a bit smelly.

There was no hot water from a tap then
and no soap powder.
They only had big bars of soap.

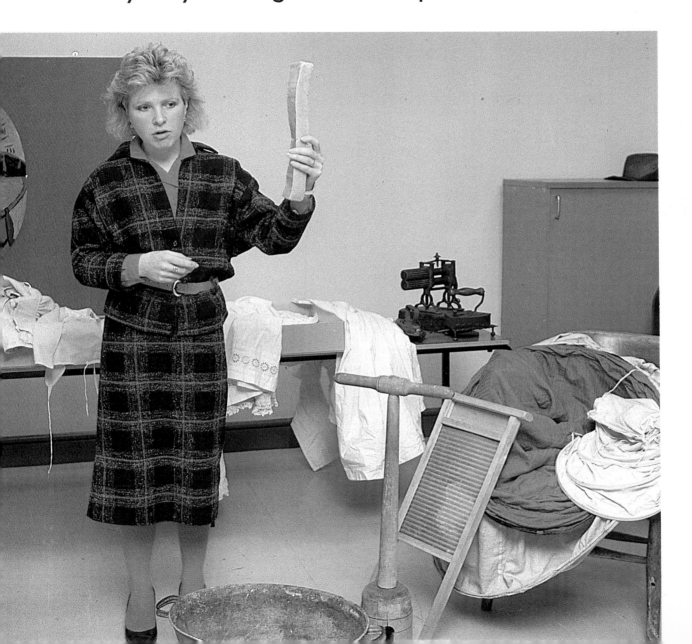

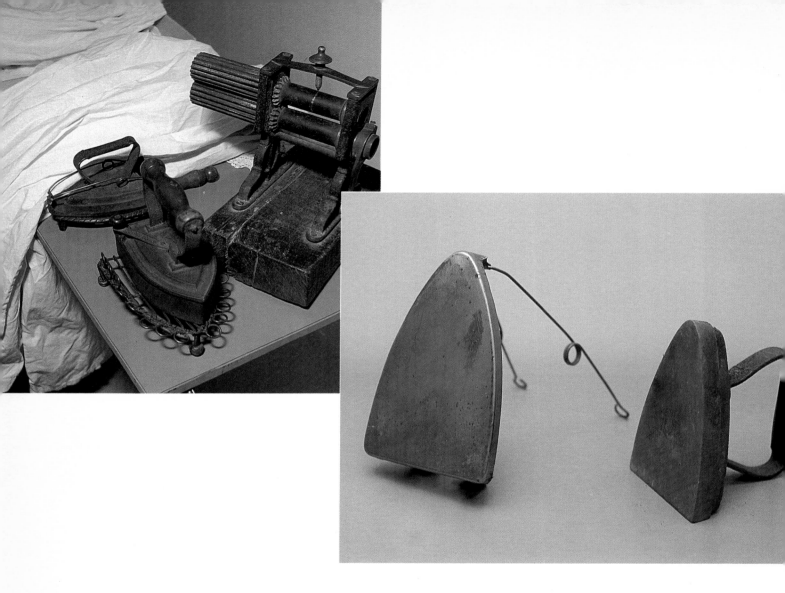

The iron had to be heated on a coal fire,
because there was no electricity.
Can you guess why it has a cover,
which can be taken off?

It took a lot of time to keep the house clean.
The vacuum cleaner had to be pumped
by hand.

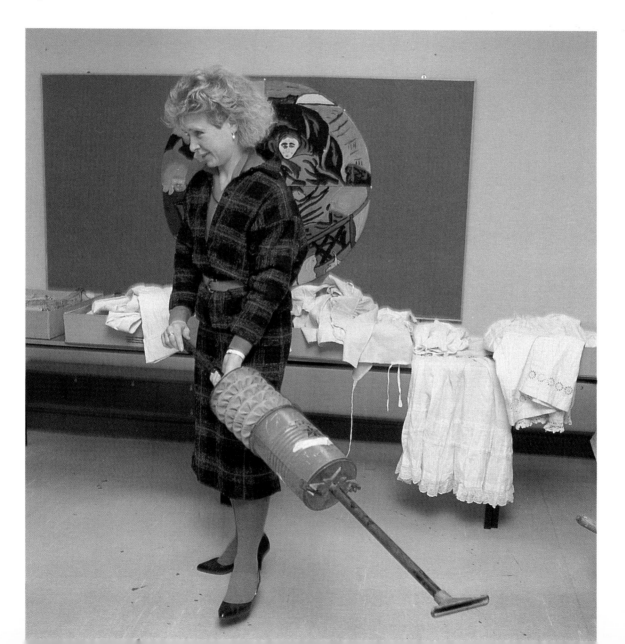

Back at school, we write
about some of the things we have seen.

Mr Rowland took
some photographs
of our visit.

They remind us
of what we saw.

Marisha and Simone
are painting
Victorian ladies.

Paul and Marsha
are making a model
of a Victorian house.

Mr Rowland shows us a steam engine.
This is how the first trains were pulled.
Natalie makes the whistle blow.

James is copying
the beautiful writing
on this bill
for a sewing machine.

A hundred years ago,
nearly everything was
written by hand.

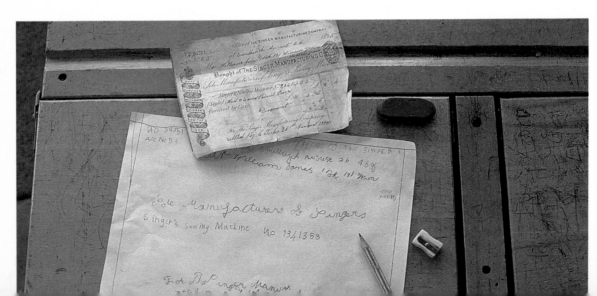

We all enjoyed our visit to the museum.
I liked dressing up best of all.

© 1987 Franklin Watts
12a Golden Square
London W1R 4BA

ISBN 0 86313 550 1

Design: Edward Kinsey

Printed in Italy
by Lito Terrazzi, Firenze

Vivien Griffiths is Head of Services to
Children and Young People,
Birmingham Public Libraries. She has
written and researched several
children's books.

The Publishers, author and
photographer would like to thank the
staff and pupils of Lee Bank Junior and
Infant School, Lee Bank, Birmingham.
Special thanks are due to Dave Brodie,
headteacher; Kevin Rowland, class
teacher and Tricia Peate, teacher with
the City of Birmingham Museum and Art
Gallery Education Service.

Slides and postcards of the paintings
shown in the book are available from:
Publications Unit, Birmingham Museum
and Art Gallery, Chamberlain Square,
Birmingham, B3 3DH.